M. A. REICHERT

SEVEN DAILY EXERCISES FOR FLUTE

OPUS 5

Edited by Carol Wincenc

Production: Joe Derhake
Covers: Cynthia Gillette
Cover photo: Christian Steiner
Music engraving: Maria Cook

LAUREN KEISER
MUSIC PUBLISHING

Carol Wincenc 21st Century Series For Flute

The Reichert *Seven Daily Exercises* (Op. 5) has long been one of the most useful, respected, and treasured learning methods written for the flute. Throughout the world everywhere I travel a mention of the exercises is met with reverence and acknowledgement of their ceaseless value-from all levels of flutists! Curiously, I who was (thankfully) brought up on a mono-diet of Taffanel-Gaubert *Daily Exercises* and Mr. Moyse's *De la Sonorité* came to Reichert's studies later in my musical development. Nonetheless, a frayed copy of Reichert's exercises still secures a permanent residence in my carry-on bag. I have seen the copies of others that have assumed the character of a personal bible with paralleled notations of accidentals not to be missed and logs of favorite tempi. Now, with pleasure I offer you this new, easier to read edition that will bring you immeasurable hours of exacting and nuanced guidance, wherever you are in your own development. The layout has been widened to let you feel the "space" that you must allow yourself in tackling these plucky exercises. I have deliberately omitted suggested metronome markings so that you can note and keep track of your particular ones. The Italian tempi markings are added to suggest speed and mood. Adapting them is vital to an expressive interpretation and your enjoyment while working. I have added the 8va symbol to encourage you to play what is written *(loco)* an octave higher.

The articulations indicated are merely suggestions. Do invent your own. The articulation samples given on page 24 can be applied to further develop your mastery of these exercises. Create fresh approaches. That goes for varying dynamics and phrasings as well. Thankfully, the way Mr. Reichert has written them, it is possible to play almost every line in a single breath, allowing you to feel and savor each key completely.

Above all, as in any technical work, awareness of the breath is crucial. Learning to breathe rapidly is a critical technique, but it needs to be tempered by a mastery of balance between conscious inhalation and exhalation. Let me suggest a routine that will work well with these exercises: Respire slowly, deeply, and amply through the nose on inhalation and in exhalation let the air stream move forward continuously to the very end of the phrase. Take time intentionally to fill up after every depletion to avoid gasping as you breathe. Taking time in this way after every depletion, we place a demand on our breathing while building endurance and confidence, making it a pleasurable experience to work on these phrases rather than being controlled by an anxiety that we might not have "enough" air. Anyone who has attended my master classes knows my echoing cue: "Healthy completion; healthy depletion; healthy completion; healthy depletion." That is why these exercises are ideal for the breathing routine I am suggesting. You can get the maximum technical work-out without struggling for air.

For example in Exercise № 5, with a lively tempo and moderate volume, it should be possible to do the eight measures in one breath. But try the breathing I have suggested: consciously take a deep and full breath before beginning, feeling the rib cage expand. Play with a richly projected sound blowing and directing the airstream continually forward. Use all the air you've drawn. Sense the thrill and beauty of the phrase written and the satisfaction of truly emptying out at its conclusion. Inhibit wanting to immediately breathe rapidly in order to go onto the next eight bar phrase and instead repeat the process described, inhaling continuously through the nose. Think of being in slow motion while inhaling if you are accustomed to breathing rapidly.

If you follow these suggested techniques for breathing, I assure you, you will find pleasure and rewards with the Reichert *Seven Daily Exercises*. They too will remain in your repertoire for a lifetime.

Carol Wincenc

Contents

DAILY EXERCISES

Edited by: Carol Wincenc

M. A. REICHERT
Op. 5

№ 1. Moderato

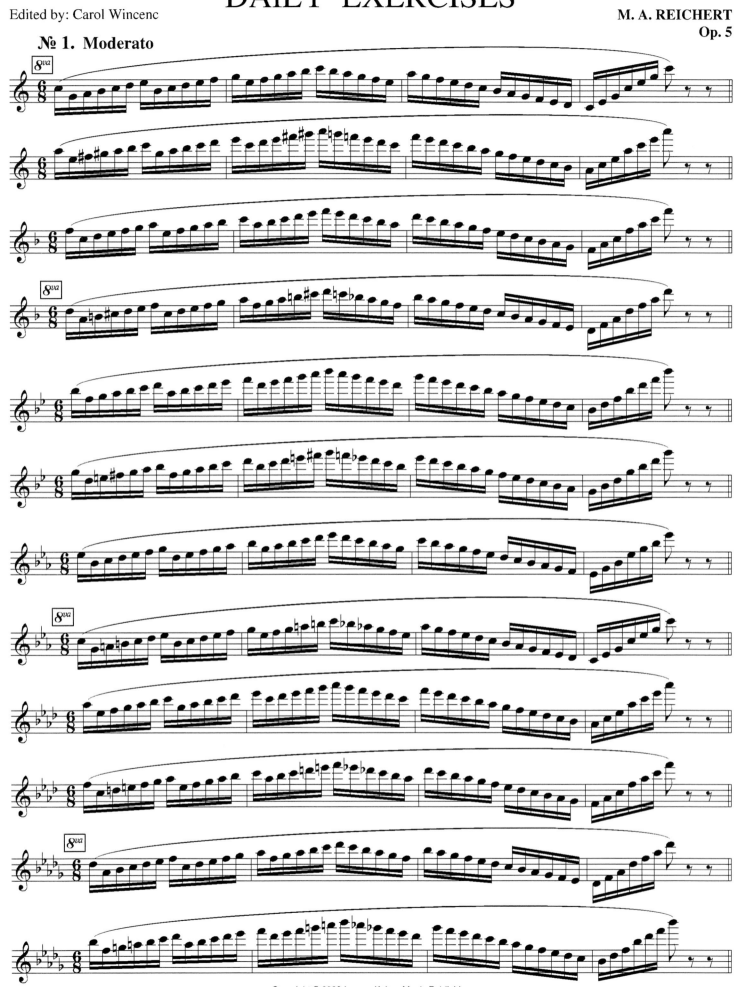

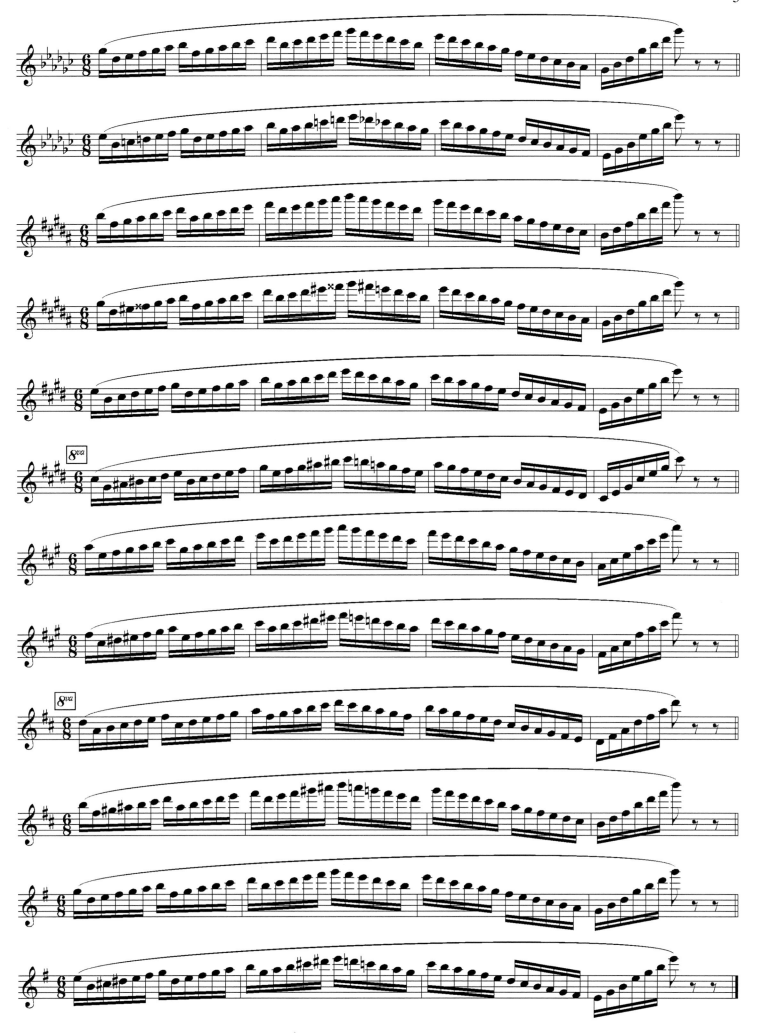

6

№ 2. Allegro

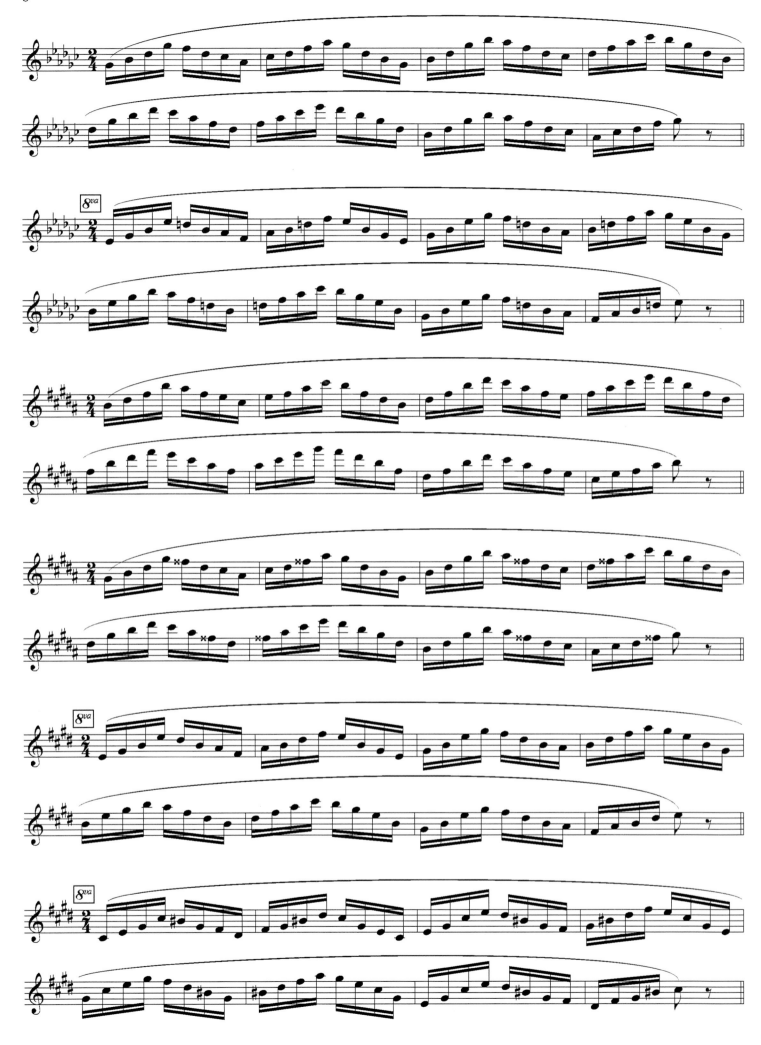

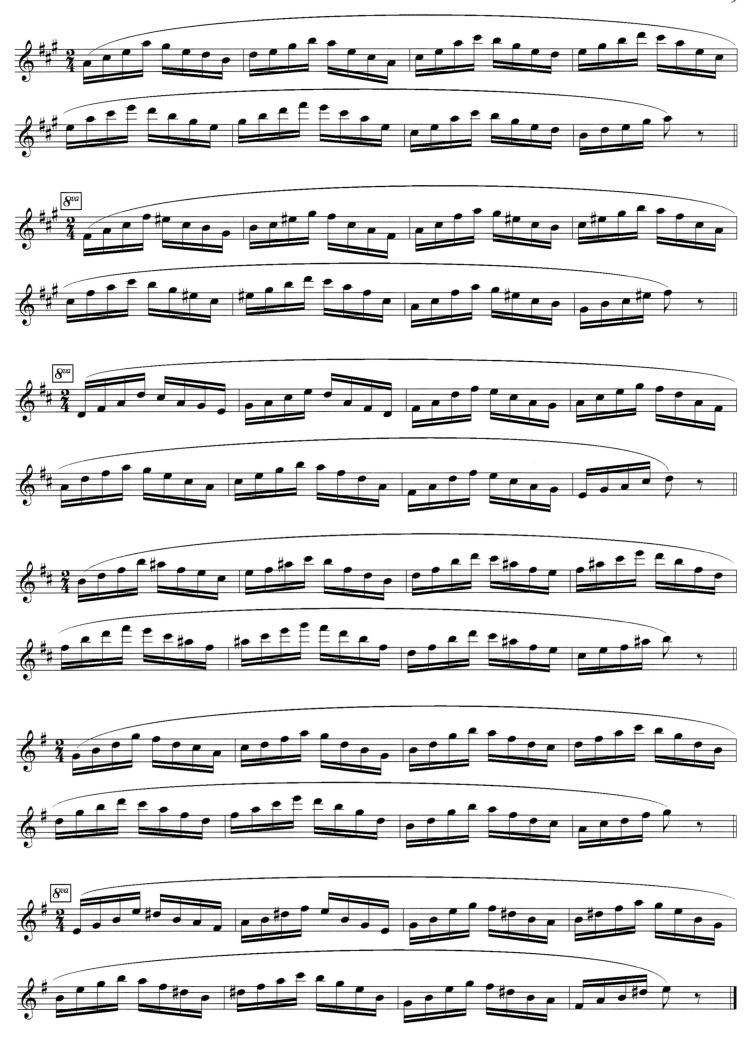

№ 3. Allegro molto

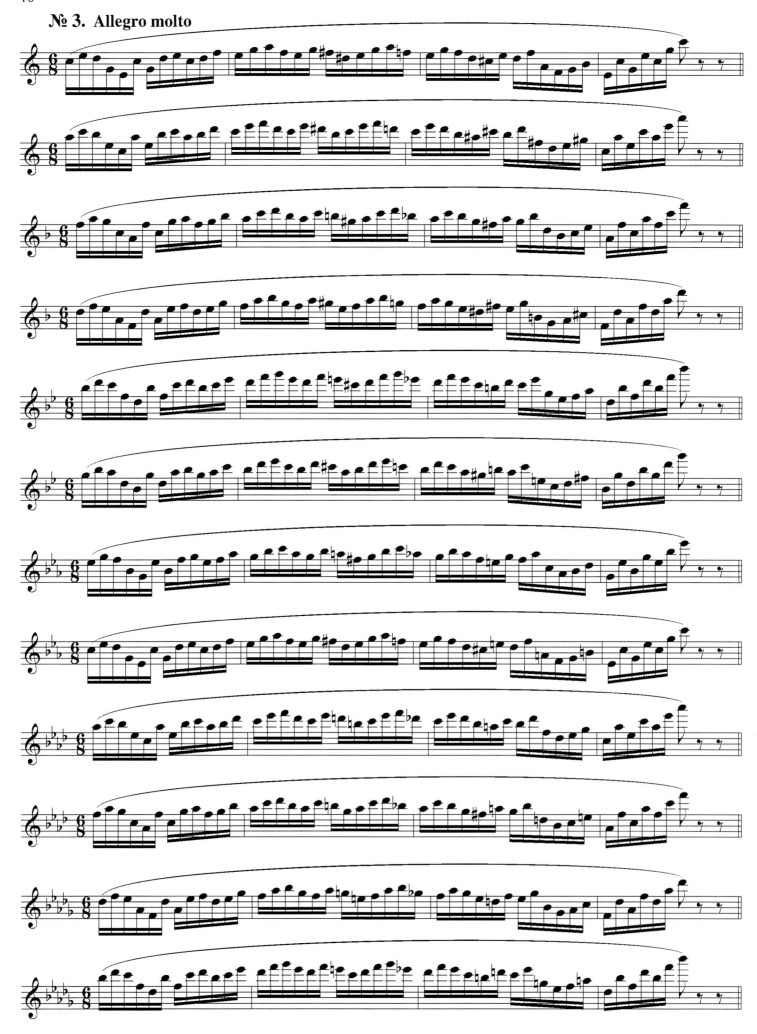

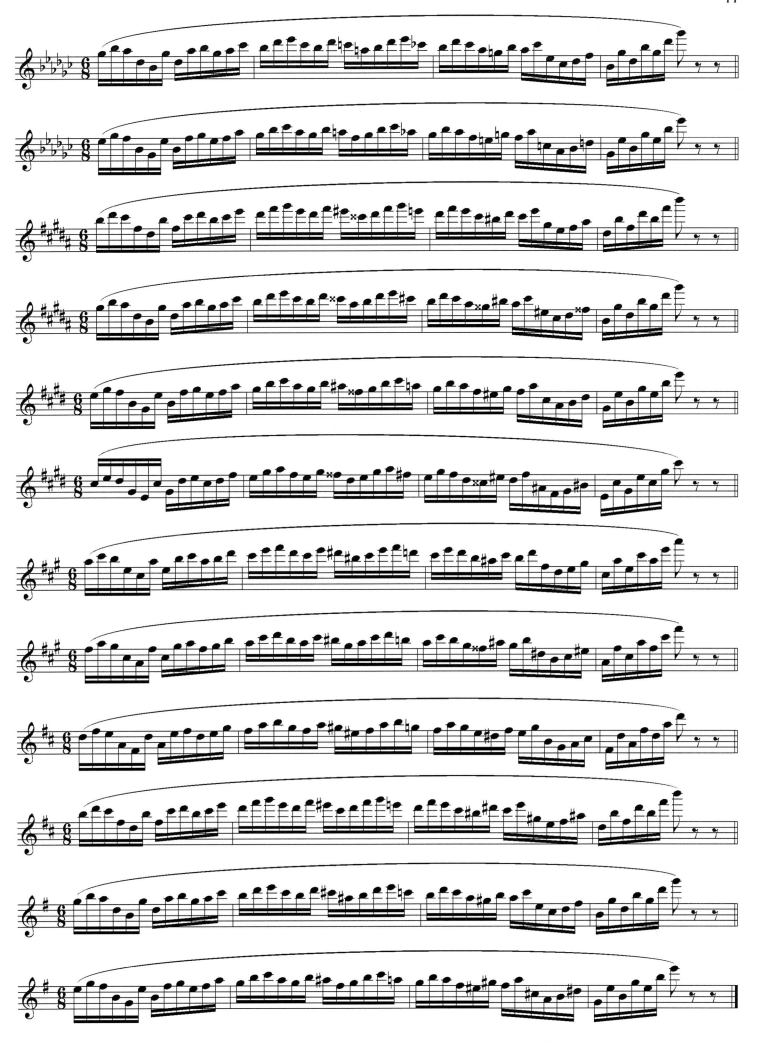

№ 4. Allegro moderato

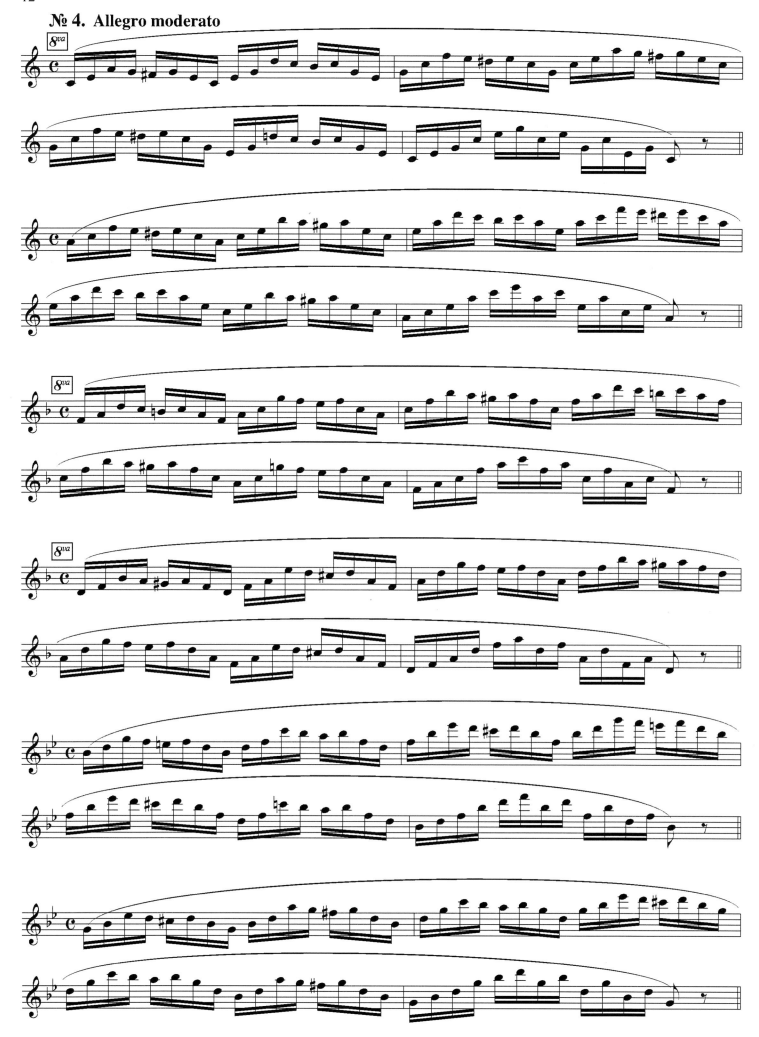

13

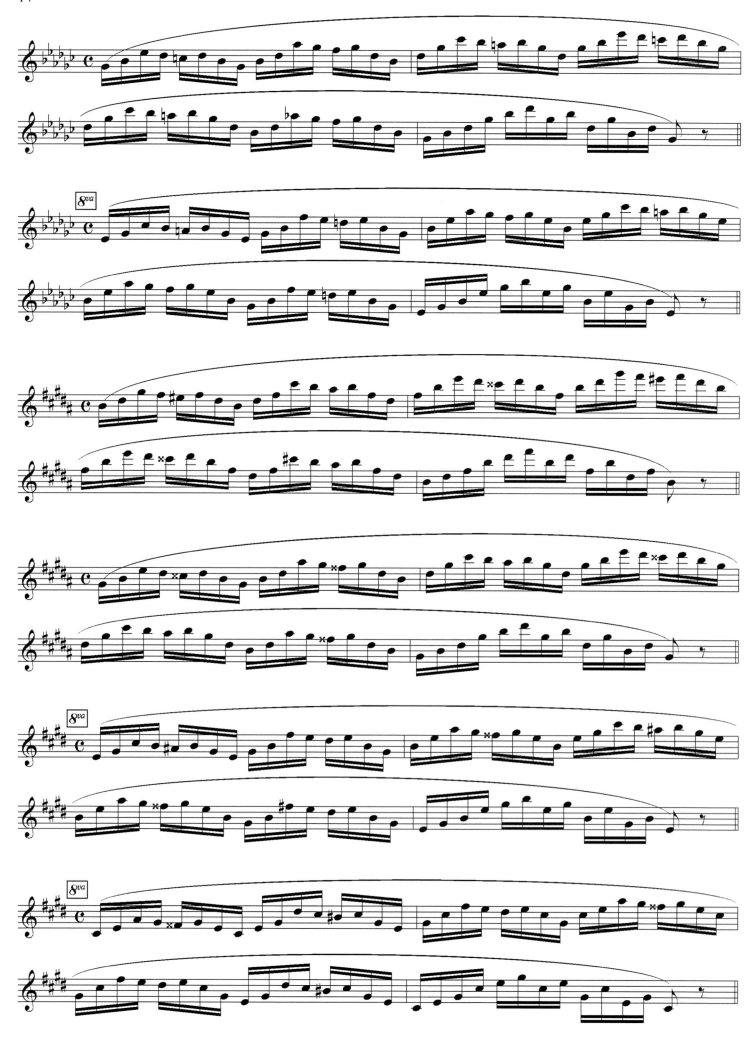

14

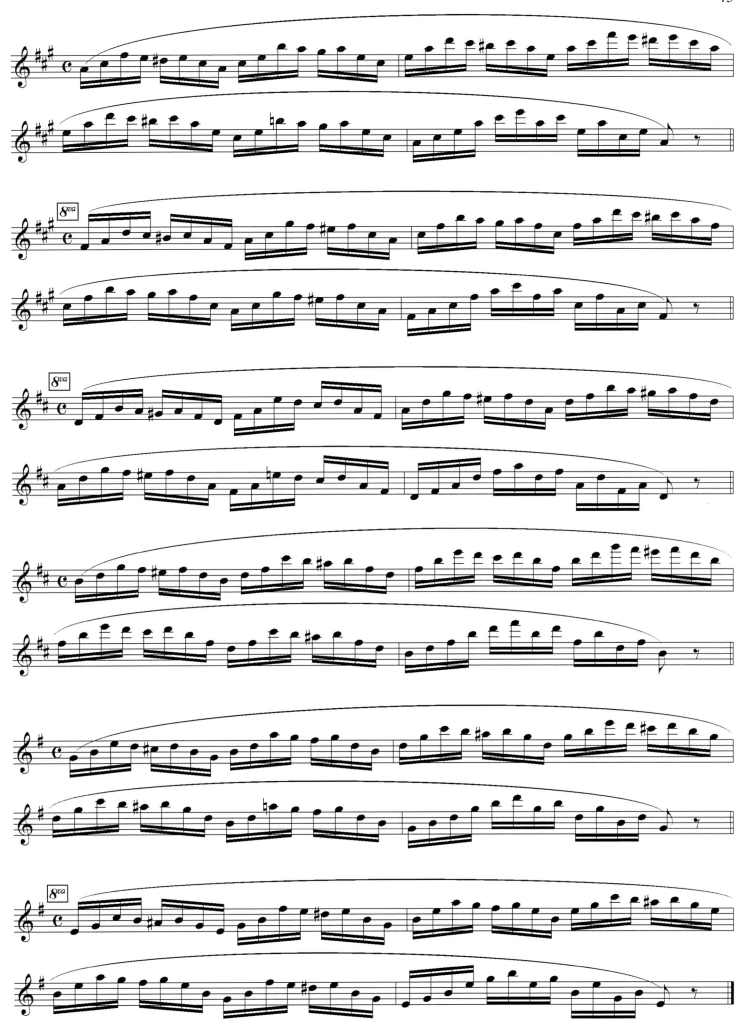

№ 5. Molto vivace

№ 6. Allegro molto

№ 7. Presto giocoso

Articulation Samples

For Exercises № 1, 3:

For Exercises № 2, 4:

For Exercises № 5, 7:

For Exercise № 6: